How to Exp.

African Bush

Simon Chapman

Badger Publishing Limited
Oldmedow Road,
Hardwick Industrial Estate,
King's Lynn PE30 4JJ
Telephone: 01438 791037

www.badgerlearning.co.uk

2 4 6 8 10 9 7 5 3 1

How to Explore the African Bush ISBN 978-1-78464-006-4

Text © Simon Chapman 2014

Complete work © Badger Publishing Limited 2014

Publisher: Susan Ross
Senior Editor: Danny Pearson
Publishing Assistant: Claire Morgan
Designer: Fiona Grant
Series Consultant: Dee Reid

Photos: Cover Image: WestEnd61/REX
Page 5: Image Broker/REX
Page 6: © Hemis/Alamy
Page 7: Image Broker/REX
Page 8: Simon Chapman
Page 9: Simon Chapman
Page 10: Simon Chapman
Page 11: FLPA/REX
Page 12: © AfriPics.com/Alamy
Page 13: Gary Roberts/REX
Page 14: Richard Du Toit/Nature Pictu/REX
Page 15: Tony Heald/Nature Picture Li/REX
Page 16: © H Lansdown/Alamy
Page 17: FLPA/REX
Page 18: WestEnd61/REX
Page 19: Simon Chapman
Page 20: © Tom Gilks/Alamy
Page 21: © willie sator/Alamy
Page 22: © Images of Africa Photobank/Alamy
Page 24: © Anthony Roberts/Alamy
Page 25: © Eric Nathan/Alamy
Page 26: F1 Online/REX
Page 27: FLPA/REX
Page 28: © Kjersti Joergensen/Alamy
Page 29: Simon Chapman
Page 30: Simon Chapman

Attempts to contact all copyright holders have been made.
If any omitted would care to contact Badger Learning, we will be happy to make appropriate arrangements.

Contents

Vocabulary

binoculars	predators
downwind	spoor
eyeshine	urine
hyena	vulture

You are in the middle of the African bush.

You can see vultures flying above you in the sky. You can hear some baboons making a lot of noise in the trees.

All around you are animal tracks – and dried up animal poo.

Today you are going to track a rhino.

1. What you need

The best places in Africa to find animals like elephants, rhino and lions are in the national parks.

These are areas that have been set aside for wildlife.

You will need a guide, who will take you around the park in a four-wheel drive and help you find the wildlife.

What to take

Light clothes for the hot days and warmer clothes for the evenings, which can get cold. You will also need:

- a sun hat
- a water bottle
- binoculars
- a torch for spotting animals at night (a head torch is best)
- camping gear

2. Checking out a waterhole

The best place to find wildlife is by a waterhole.

In the African bush there are many months when there is no rain at all and most mammals need to drink at least once a day.

So if you sit still and wait, you will see animals coming to the waterhole.

The animals will have a drink, then hurry off before the predators arrive.

First thing in the morning you might see kudu, antelope and zebra drinking at the waterhole.

Later in the day you might spot giraffe or buffalo coming for a drink.

In the evening you might see a herd of elephants having a drink.

If you are lucky, you might even see a lion!

The roar of a lion can be
heard up to five miles away.

Spotlighting

If you shine your torch at the waterhole at night you might see pairs of eyes glowing back at you.

Animals who come to the waterhole at night are good at seeing in the dark.

Their eyes are very shiny and reflect your torchlight.

This is called eyeshine.

WOW! facts

Lions have yellow eyeshine
and zebra have green/blue eyeshine.

3. Staking out a kill

Another way to find wildlife is to find where there has been a kill.

Predators like lions are often quite hard to spot as they spend much of the time out of sight, hunting for prey like antelope.

But when one lion kills an antelope, other lions will crowd in for a share of the carcass.

The trick to finding where a lion has killed an antelope is to look out for where vultures land.

If you are lucky, you might find hyenas eating the bits of flesh the lions have left behind.

But even if most of the flesh has been taken, you will often find vultures and jackals fighting for the scraps that are left.

Lions rip open the skin to eat the soft flesh underneath.

They eat the best bits.

Vultures will put their whole heads right into the carcass to pull out tasty morsels.

Hyenas will crunch bones for the marrow inside.

Jackals hang around the edges and snatch what they can.

4. Tracking on foot

Tracking big animals like rhino on foot is a lot scarier than watching them from a safari truck.

It's a good idea to set out very early in the morning when more animals are moving around.

You must move quietly and look out for the signs
that show which animals have passed by recently.

If there has been no rain for weeks, there can be so many footprints in the dust that it can be hard to tell which animals are around.

Look at animal poo on the ground. Break it open with your fingers.

If the 'spoor' (this is what trackers call the poo) is still a bit wet the animal will probably be nearby.

1. Broken branches

This shows you big animals have passed by.

Look carefully at the size of the gap and how high branches are snapped.

This will be a clue to how big the animal is.

2. Claw marks on tree trunks

These show if lions have been nearby.

Look carefully at the ground. You might be able to see the paw prints where the lion has stood on its hind legs to scratch the tree.

3. A stinky smell of urine

This is a good sign that animals have been nearby.

Lots of animals spray their urine in the leaves of bushes.

When other animals smell the urine they can tell who has been there. They can also read a message in the smell.

The message might be:
- Hello! I'm looking for a mate.
- Get off! This is my patch!
- I want to be boss around here.
- I'm getting old and cranky so leave me alone.

Tracking tips

If you want to track rhino on foot, you will have to get used to looking closely at animal poo.

If you are on the trail of a black rhino, you will see twigs in the 12 centimetre long poo.

This is because black rhino eat leaves and then the twigs come out in their poo.

If you are on the trail of a white rhino, you will see grass in the poo because white rhino eat grass.

WOW! facts

White and black rhino are both the same colour: grey.

Black rhino

- Smaller than a white rhino.
- Its mouth is shaped like a hook.
- It is usually found on its own.
- It is very bad-tempered!

White rhino

- Can be twice the size of a black rhino.
- Its mouth is very flat.
- It is usually found in herds.
- It is not very bad-tempered (but it will still attack humans!).

5. Close up

It is dusk in the African bush and you're on the trail of a rhino.

You have seen rhino tracks in the dust.

You have found rhino poo that is still wet.

You see that some branches on the trees have been snapped off.

You can smell stinky urine.

Then you see something moving in the trees ahead.

Check which way the wind is blowing.

If it is blowing from you towards an animal (you are 'upwind'), it will smell you and probably move away.

If you are 'downwind' of it, you can take a chance and get really close.

But you must be very quiet and stay out of sight.

Wait!

How close do you want to get?

A black rhino can run at nearly 30 miles per hour, and weighs one and a half tonnes!

Do you really want to get up close and personal with an angry black rhino?

Floodlit waterhole
mother Black Rhino
and young drinking.
Just earlier the baby
was suckling.
Right now the
Rhinos are hanging
back and a bull
elephant has come
in to drink.
2 jackals walked
across foreground.
A third rhino has
just arrived.

7.50

The dark pool perfectly
reflects.

Male just had
brief stand off with female — She bellowed then
turned her back

Questions

Name something you should take with you to the African bush. *(page 7)*

Where is the best place to find wildlife? *(page 8)*

How far away can you hear a lion's roar? *(page 10)*

How can you tell there has been a kill? *(page 15)*

What is a 'spoor'? *(page 20)*

Name one difference between a black rhino and a white rhino. *(pages 26-27)*

Index